backstreet boys

backstreet boys

Album Art: ©1997 Zomba Recording Corporation
Album Art Direction: Jackie Murphy/Nick Gamma
Photography: Eli Hershko

Project Manager: Jeannette DeLisa
Art Layout: Marcela Perez

BACRSTREE

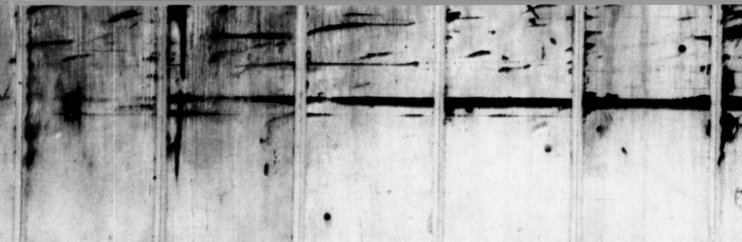

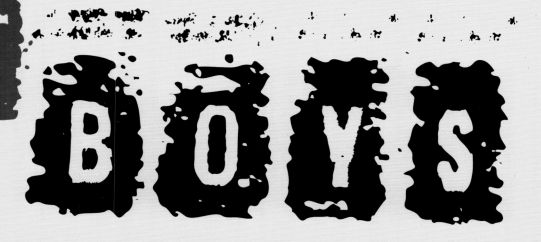

T BOYS

CONTENTS

QUIT PLAYING GAMES

(With My Heart)

By
MAX MARTIN and
HERBIE CRICHLOW

Moderate rock ♩ = 104

§ *Verse:*

1. E - ven in my heart,____ I____ see

2.3. *See additional lyrics*

you're not be - in' true to me.____ Deep with - in my soul____ I____

Quit Playing Games - 5 - 1
PF9731

Verse 2:
I live my life the way,
To keep you comin' back to me.
Everything I do is for you,
So what is it that you can't see?
Sometimes I wish I could turn back time,
Impossible as it may seem.
But I wish I could so bad, baby
You better quit playing games with my heart.
(To Chorus:)

Verse 3:
(Measures 1-8 instrumental solo ad lib.)
Sometimes I wish I could turn back time,
Impossible as it may seem.
But I wish I could so bad, baby.
Quit playing games with my heart.
(To Coda)

WE'VE GOT IT GOIN' ON

By
MAX MARTIN, DENNIZ POP
and HERBIE CRICHLOW

We've got it go - in'___ on___ for years.___

We've got it go - in'___ on___

for years.___

Spoken: *Well, I'm creepin' up on your left, straight up funky when I get with you.*

I get ruthless when I get wet, keep the party packed in my corner. Tough like granite to keep the crowd hype,

16

AS LONG AS YOU LOVE ME

By
MAX MARTIN

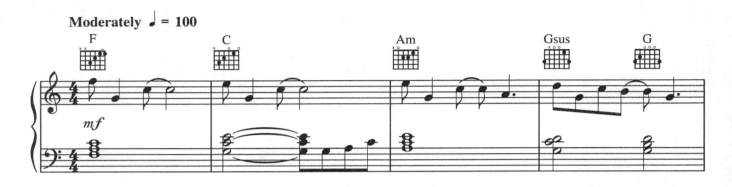

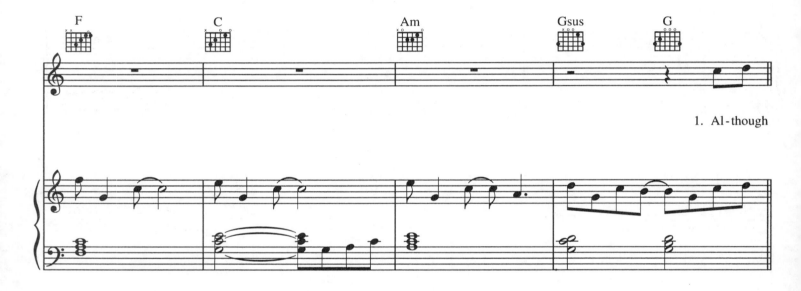

1. Al-though

Verse 1:

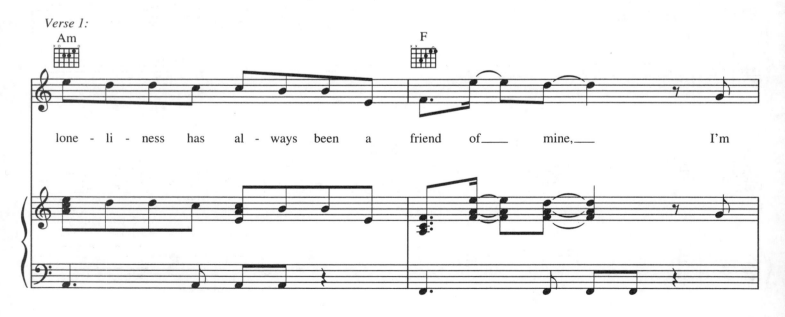

lone - li - ness has al - ways been a friend of___ mine,___ I'm

24

ALL I HAVE TO GIVE

By
FULL FORCE

26

ANYWHERE FOR YOU

By
WAYNE PERRY and
GARY BAKER

Moderately slow ♩ = 76

I'd go an-y-where_ for you,_ an-y-where you asked_ me to,_____ I'd do an-y-thing_ for you,_ an-y-thing you want_ me to._____

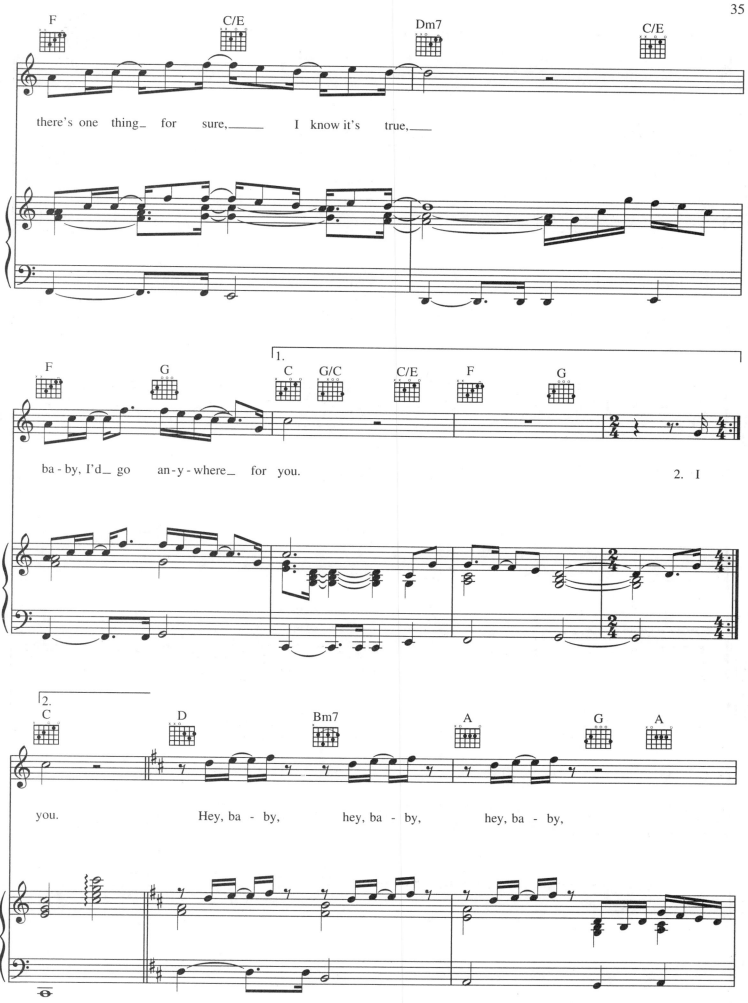

there's one thing_ for sure,____ I know it's true,____

ba - by, I'd_ go an-y-where_ for you.

2. I

you. Hey, ba - by, hey, ba - by, hey, ba - by,

Verse 2:
I used to think that dreams
Were just for sentimental fools,
And I'd never find someone
Who'd give their love so true.
But I knew the very minute,
Couldn't live my life without you in it,
And now I want the whole wide world
To know.
(To Chorus:)

HEY, MR. DJ
(Keep Playin' This Song)

By
TIMMY ALLEN, LARRY "ROCK" CAMPBELL
and JOLYON SKINNER

Moderately ♩ = 96

Verse:

1. I could tell when I stepped in the room and I saw you stand-ing there,
2. Now it feels like it could be ro-mance as we dance a-cross the floor.

Hey, Mr. DJ - 9 - 1
PF9731

by the rhy-thm of your bod - y and the mu - sic in your eyes.___

___ I was lost___ in - side your world___ with you,___

oo, oo, oo, oo, oo.___

Chorus:

Hey, Mis - ter D___ J, keep play - ing this song___ for me.

42

44

Chorus:

Hey, Mis - ter D J, play that song for me.

Hey, Mis - ter D____ J, keep play - ing this song____ for me.

Out on the floor____ in my arms____ she's got - ta be.

Let's get it on,____ jam all night long.____ Mis - ter D__

Hey, Mr. DJ - 9 - 7
PF9731

___ J, Mis - ter D ___ J, play it, ___ play ___ it for ___ me, D ___ J.

Em

Keep it cool, Mis-ter D   J,   keep it cool, Mis-ter D   J.

Repeat ad lib. and fade

Keep it cool, Mis-ter D   J,   keep it cool, Mis-ter D   J.

I'LL NEVER BREAK YOUR HEART

By
ALBERT MANNO and
EUGENE WILDE

Slowly ♩. = 66

B♭   Gm   E♭maj7

Spoken: Baby, I know you are hurting; right now you feel like you could never love again. Now all I ask is for a chance

Verse:

F   E♭   F   B♭   Gm

to prove that I love you. 1. From the first day that I saw_ your smil-ing face,_ hon-ey, I
2. *See additional lyrics*

E♭   F   E♭   F

knew_ that we would be to-geth-er for-ev-er. Ooh, when I

Repeat and fade

die than live with-out you, I'll give you all of me, hon-ey, that's no lie. I'll nev-er

break your_____ heart,____ I'll nev-er make you_____ cry.___ I'd rath-er

die than live with-out you, I'll give you all of me, hon-ey, that's no lie. I'll nev-er

Verse 2:
As I walked by you,
Will you get to know me
A little more better?
Girl, that's the way love goes.
And I know you're afraid
To let your feelings show,
And I understand.
But girl, it's time to let go.

I deserve a try, honey,
Just once,
Give me a chance
And I'll prove this all wrong.
You walked in,
You were so quick to judge,
But honey, he's nothing like me.
Darling, why can't you see?
(To Chorus:)

DARLIN'

By
TIMMY ALLEN and
NNEKA MORTON

Girl, you should know I love you by now, there's so many ways to love,

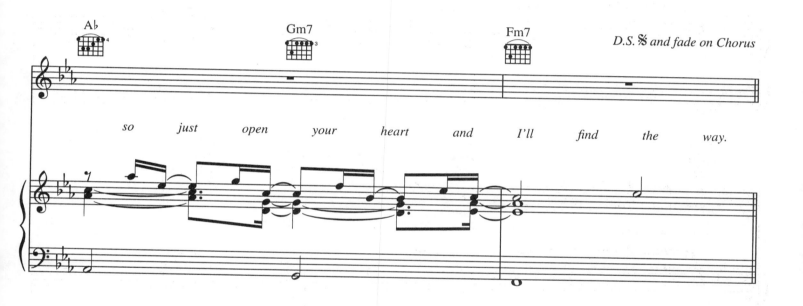

D.S. % and fade on Chorus

so just open your heart and I'll find the way.

Verse 2:
If your eyes had a reason
When they won't turn away from me,
They're trying to hide all truth you might say.
If you listen to me, girl,
If you know how I'm feeling inside,
Then maybe you wouldn't shut me out your life, baby.
(To Chorus:)

GET DOWN
(You're the One for Me)

By
BÜELENT ARIS and
TONI COTTURA

Moderate funk rock ♩ = 116

You're the one for me, you're my ec-sta-cy, you're the one I need.

Get down, get down and

60

I feel in heav-en when I look in your eyes,__ I know that you are the one__

__ for me. You drive me cra-zy 'cause you're one of a kind,__ *To Coda*

Chorus:

I want your lov-ing and I want it right now. Get down, get down and

move it all a-round. Get down, get down and move it all a-round.__ Get

N.C.

Rap: Bang bang bang, here we come, here we slam,   it's the fun factory with the B. S. B's.

Get on your knees, tryin' to scream or touch me please.   Back Street Boys, are you with it, A.J. hit it!

Come   on,   girl,   and   get   down,   smack it up, flip it and move it all around.

2. D#7   D.S. 𝄋 al Coda

Here it is, you wanna get with this, put you at the top of my list.

SET ADRIFT ON MEMORY BLISS

Words and Music by
ATTRELL CORDES and
GARY KEMP

Verse 2:

G

2. Des - ti - ny___ is ev - 'ry - thing, re - al - i - ty's re - placed you with the

F

big - gest emp - ty void__ I've ev - er had___ in life.___

G

Bet you say that I don't care, I bet you say that I don't e - ven

F

think of___ you, but God knows how wrong___ you are.___

IF YOU WANT IT TO BE GOOD GIRL

(Get Yourself a Bad Boy)

By
R.J. LANGE

74

EVERYBODY
(BACKSTREET'S BACK)

Words and Music by
DENNIZ POP and
MAX MARTIN

♩ = 108

Ev-'ry-bo-dy ___ rock your bo-dy. ___ Ev-'ry-

-bo-dy ___ rock your bo-dy right. ___ Back-street's back al-right!

Hey ___ yeah! ___ Now! ___

Everybody (Backstreet's Back) - 5 - 1
PF9731

1. Oh my God we're back a-gain,_____ bro-thers, sis- ters ev-'ry-bo -dy sing - in'_____
(Verse 2 see block lyric)

Tacet 2°

_____ gon-na bring the fla - vour, show you how._____ Got-ta

ques-tion for___ you, bet-ter ans- wer now._____ Am I o-ri-gi-nal?___

(Yeah._____) Am I the on- ly one?___ (Yeah._____) Am I

Verse 2:
Now throw your hands up in the air
And wave 'em around like you just don't care
If you wanna party let me hear you yell
'Cos we got it going on again.

Am I original …